PRINCEWILL LAGANG

Qatar's Golden Sands: A Tale of Opulence and Intrigue

First published by PRINCEWILL LAGANG 2023

Copyright © 2023 by Princewill Lagang

All rights reserved. No part of this publication may be reproduced, stored or transmitted in any form or by any means, electronic, mechanical, photocopying, recording, scanning, or otherwise without written permission from the publisher. It is illegal to copy this book, post it to a website, or distribute it by any other means without permission.

Princewill Lagang asserts the moral right to be identified as the author of this work.

First edition

This book was professionally typeset on Reedsy.
Find out more at reedsy.com

Contents

1. Qatar's Golden Sands: A Tale of Opulence and Intrigue — 1
2. Sands of History - Qatar's Ancient Roots — 4
3. Pearls, Pirates, and Power Struggles — 6
4. The Modern Mirage - Qatar's Transformation Begins — 8
5. Building a Cultural Oasis - Qatar's Global Ambitions — 11
6. The Diplomatic Dance - Qatar's Role in Regional and Global... — 14
7. Challenges and Controversies - Qatar's Path to Sustainable... — 17
8. Qatar's Vision for the Future - Navigating Uncertainties — 20
9. Qatar's Place in a Globalized World - Challenges and... — 23
10. Shaping the Future - Qatar's Legacy and Beyond — 25
11. Qatar's Global Impact - A Beacon of Hope and Progress — 28
12. A Vision Realized - Qatar's Enduring Legacy — 30
13. Summary — 32

1

Qatar's Golden Sands: A Tale of Opulence and Intrigue

In the heart of the Arabian Peninsula, where the unforgiving desert meets the azure waters of the Persian Gulf, there lies a land of wealth and mystique. This is a tale of Qatar, a tiny nation that has risen from obscurity to become a beacon of opulence and intrigue in the modern world.

Qatar, a name that once conjured images of endless sand dunes and nomadic tribes, now resonates with a different narrative—a story of boundless riches, architectural marvels, and geopolitical maneuvering. This chapter delves into the captivating tapestry of a nation that has transformed itself from a modest pearl fishing community into a global powerhouse, all in the span of a few decades.

The origins of Qatar's journey to opulence and intrigue can be traced back to its discovery of oil in the mid-20th century. Before the vast reservoirs of black gold were unearthed, Qatar was a humble land of pearl divers and traders, its people eking out a modest living from the bounties of the Gulf. The pearl trade was the lifeblood of the nation, but it was a precarious one, for the riches of the sea were fickle, and the scorching desert offered little respite from the harsh realities of life.

Then, in 1939, oil was discovered beneath the Qatari sands, setting in motion a transformation that would alter the course of the nation's history. The once-nomadic inhabitants of this land suddenly found themselves stewards of vast wealth, as oil revenues began to flow into the coffers of the Qatari government. The tiny peninsula, no larger than the state of Connecticut, became a veritable treasure trove.

Qatar's newfound wealth did not go unnoticed. The world's major powers cast their eyes upon this emerging player in the global energy market. It was a time of intrigue, as Qatar navigated the treacherous waters of international politics and diplomacy, seeking to protect its interests and assert its presence on the world stage. The tiny nation found itself at the crossroads of regional rivalries and global power struggles, as nations jostled for influence in the Gulf.

As the first chapter unfolds, we see the rise of Qatar's visionary leaders, who recognized the potential of their nation's newfound riches. They charted a course that would see Qatar transformed from a sleepy desert enclave into a thriving metropolis of glass and steel, a testament to the limitless ambitions of its people. The emergence of Doha, the nation's capital, as a glittering jewel in the Arabian Peninsula, showcases Qatar's determination to embrace modernity while preserving its cultural heritage.

But opulence and intrigue often go hand in hand, and Qatar's rise was not without controversy. The story of the nation's pursuit of the 2022 FIFA World Cup is one that captures the attention of the world and raises questions about the lengths to which a nation will go to secure its place on the global stage. Allegations of corruption and concerns over labor rights have shrouded this ambitious endeavor in a cloud of controversy.

QATAR'S GOLDEN SANDS: A TALE OF OPULENCE AND INTRIGUE

In this chapter, we journey through the dazzling cityscape of Doha, with its iconic skyscrapers, opulent shopping malls, and world-class museums. We explore the aspirations of a nation that has leveraged its wealth to become a global cultural hub, attracting luminaries from around the world.

We also delve into the intricate web of Qatari diplomacy and alliances, as the nation seeks to navigate the shifting sands of regional politics. Qatar's involvement in the Arab Spring, its support for various rebel groups in the Middle East, and its complex relationship with neighboring countries have all contributed to the intrigue that surrounds this small but influential nation.

"Qatar's Golden Sands: A Tale of Opulence and Intrigue" is a narrative that weaves together the threads of history, politics, and culture to tell the captivating story of a nation that has risen from the desert sands to captivate the world's imagination. As we embark on this journey, we'll explore the contradictions and complexities of a nation at the crossroads of tradition and modernity, opulence and intrigue, and the relentless pursuit of a place in the sun.

2

Sands of History - Qatar's Ancient Roots

To truly understand the opulence and intrigue of modern Qatar, one must first explore the deep sands of its history, where the roots of this nation lie buried beneath layers of time and tradition. Chapter 2 delves into the ancient heritage that has shaped the Qatari identity, offering a rich tapestry of narratives that provide context to the remarkable transformation of this tiny Gulf state.

Qatar's history is a tale of resilience, adaptability, and the interplay of diverse influences. Long before oil gushed from the earth, and before the glittering skyscrapers of Doha pierced the sky, the Qatari people were a seafaring and trading community, intimately connected with the waters of the Persian Gulf.

The earliest known inhabitants of the Qatari peninsula were the Bedouin tribes and coastal fishermen who embraced a nomadic way of life. They navigated the harsh desert landscapes and the azure waters of the Gulf, surviving by pearl diving, fishing, and the trading of goods. These humble beginnings laid the groundwork for Qatar's future as a trading hub.

In antiquity, the region that is now Qatar was an essential stop on the maritime trade routes that connected the Far East, the Indian subcontinent, and the Arabian Peninsula. The ancient port city of Al Zubarah, which thrived from the late 18th century to the early 19th century, was a testament to Qatar's historical significance as a trading center. The UNESCO World Heritage Site stands as a silent witness to the bustling markets, pearling industry, and cultural exchanges that once characterized the region.

Through the chapters of history, Qatar was influenced by various empires and entities, including the Persians, the Ottomans, and the British. These foreign powers left their indelible marks on the culture, governance, and commerce of the Qatari people. The signing of treaties with the British in the late 19th and early 20th centuries marked the beginning of a new era, transforming Qatar into a British protectorate and laying the foundation for its modern statehood.

Independence, however, was not an easy feat. Qatar faced turbulent times in the early 20th century, marked by tribal conflicts and regional tensions. It was only in the mid-20th century that the nation began to emerge from its turbulent past, partly due to the discovery of oil and the visionary leadership that recognized the potential of this newfound resource.

As we traverse the sands of history, we encounter colorful characters, tribal rivalries, and the enduring spirit of the Qatari people. We learn of the emergence of the Al Thani dynasty, which continues to rule Qatar to this day. The journey through time reveals the complex and interconnected threads of Qatar's heritage, reflecting the rich diversity of its population, from the Bedouin tribes of the interior to the seafaring communities along the coast.

Chapter 2 lays the foundation for the opulent and intriguing Qatar we know today. It is a reminder that beneath the glittering façade of modernity, there exists a historical tapestry that has contributed to the nation's unique identity, enriching the narrative of Qatar's journey from humble beginnings to a global powerhouse.

3

Pearls, Pirates, and Power Struggles

In the evolving narrative of Qatar's journey from obscurity to opulence, Chapter 3 uncovers the mesmerizing tales of pearls, pirates, and power struggles that once shaped the destiny of this tiny Gulf nation. As we delve into the annals of history, we encounter the stories of daring pearl divers, ruthless pirates, and the relentless pursuit of influence by foreign powers.

The Qatari coastlines, bathed by the warm waters of the Persian Gulf, have long been renowned for the pearls they yielded. Pearling was the economic backbone of Qatar for centuries, drawing not only the country's own inhabitants but also divers from around the region to its shores. The pearling season, a perilous and labor-intensive endeavor, was a ritual etched into the cultural fabric of the nation, marking the rhythm of life for its people.

As Chapter 3 unfolds, we follow the pearl divers as they ventured into the depths of the Gulf, seeking the elusive treasures of the sea. These divers, often holding their breath for minutes at a time, navigated the perilous waters, contending with the risk of shark attacks and drowning, all for the promise of the lustrous pearls that would eventually adorn the jewelry of the world's elite.

Pearls brought wealth, and wealth, in turn, brought power. The stories of pearl merchants and traders, who established economic ties that stretched from the Gulf to the Indian subcontinent, reveal the interconnectedness of the region's trade routes. These merchants cultivated a reputation for their shrewd business acumen, their entrepreneurial spirit a precursor to the modern-day economic ambitions of Qatar.

However, the azure waters that offered riches also attracted a different breed of opportunists—pirates. The chapter unfolds tales of daring pirate raids and skirmishes, as seafaring outlaws sought to plunder the wealth amassed from Qatar's pearling industry. These maritime conflicts, coupled with the vagaries of nature, cast a shadow of uncertainty over the pearl trade, further highlighting the precarious nature of life on the Qatari coast.

The thirst for power was not confined to pirates alone. Foreign powers, notably the British and Ottomans, recognized the strategic importance of the Gulf and vied for control of the region. As a result, Qatar became embroiled in the power struggles of these empires, with shifting allegiances and treaties that would have far-reaching consequences in the future.

In this chapter, we explore the alliances and allegiances that the Qatari leaders forged with these foreign powers, particularly with the British, who extended their protection over Qatar. These treaties marked a pivotal juncture in Qatar's history, setting the stage for the emergence of the nation as a modern state.

"Pearls, Pirates, and Power Struggles" is a chapter that encapsulates the trials and tribulations that Qatar faced in its quest for prosperity. The stories of pearl divers, pirate raids, and diplomatic intrigue reveal the resilience and resourcefulness of a nation that, even in the face of adversity, laid the foundation for the opulent and intriguing Qatar we know today.

4

The Modern Mirage - Qatar's Transformation Begins

In this chapter, we delve into the pivotal era when Qatar's modern transformation commenced in earnest, as the discovery of oil and visionary leadership reshaped the nation and set it on the path to becoming a global powerhouse. It's a story of ambition, innovation, and strategic thinking that has continued to define Qatar's journey from modest beginnings to opulence.

The mid-20th century marked a turning point for Qatar as black gold, in the form of oil, was discovered beneath its deserts. This chapter takes us back to the momentous day in 1939 when oil reserves were struck, changing the course of the nation's history forever. The black liquid that flowed from the earth held the promise of unimaginable wealth, sparking a rush of excitement and hope among the Qatari people.

The sudden influx of oil revenues transformed the tiny, humble nation of Qatar into a player on the global energy stage. We explore how visionary leaders recognized the potential of this newfound resource and set in motion a series of initiatives to harness it for the nation's benefit. These leaders, including Sheikh Jassim bin Mohammed Al Thani and Sheikh Hamad bin Khalifa Al Thani, played a pivotal role in shaping Qatar's destiny.

Chapter 4 delves into the careful planning and investment in infrastructure and human capital that were instrumental in Qatar's rapid development. We examine the establishment of Qatar Petroleum and the nation's decision to develop its natural gas resources, a move that would make Qatar a global energy giant and a leading exporter of liquefied natural gas (LNG). The growth of Qatar's hydrocarbon sector had far-reaching consequences for the nation's economy and geopolitical significance.

As oil revenues poured into the Qatari treasury, the nation's leaders realized the importance of diversifying the economy to reduce dependence on a single commodity. We learn about the launch of the Qatar National Vision 2030, a comprehensive plan aimed at fostering sustainable development and modernization in sectors such as education, healthcare, and infrastructure. This visionary roadmap laid the foundation for Qatar's current prosperity and its ambitious aspirations for the future.

The transformation of the capital city, Doha, becomes a central focus in this chapter. We explore the rise of iconic skyscrapers, luxurious shopping malls, and world-class museums, including the Museum of Islamic Art and the National Museum of Qatar. These architectural marvels reflect Qatar's determination to embrace modernity while preserving its cultural heritage.

However, the path to prosperity was not without its challenges. The rapid pace of development brought with it questions about the sustainability of Qatar's economic growth and the treatment of its expatriate labor force, issues that would later garner international attention and scrutiny.

Chapter 4 tells the story of Qatar's ascent as an economic powerhouse, and its emergence as a dynamic, forward-looking nation on the global stage. As we explore the nation's transformation, we witness the juxtaposition of opulence and the intricate challenges that come with rapid development, setting the stage for the compelling narrative that unfolds in subsequent chapters.

5

Building a Cultural Oasis - Qatar's Global Ambitions

In Chapter 5, we continue our exploration of Qatar's remarkable journey, focusing on its aspirations to become a global cultural and intellectual hub. This chapter delves into the opulent investments made in education, the arts, and sports, revealing how the nation's leaders sought to elevate Qatar's influence on the world stage.

Qatar's quest to become a hub of knowledge and culture led to a transformative shift in the nation's educational landscape. The establishment of Education City stands as a testament to Qatar's commitment to fostering intellectual growth and innovation. We delve into the inception of Education City, a sprawling complex comprising several world-renowned universities, where students from around the world come to study and collaborate. The Qatari government's significant investments in education have not only attracted top-tier institutions but have also created opportunities for Qatar's own young talent to receive a world-class education.

Education City is home to branch campuses of renowned institutions like

Georgetown University, Carnegie Mellon University, and Northwestern University, offering a diverse array of programs, from liberal arts to engineering. We explore the dynamic environment of Education City, where innovation and cross-cultural exchange thrive, and the boundaries of knowledge are constantly being pushed.

This chapter also takes us into Qatar's commitment to preserving and promoting its cultural heritage. Qatar's leaders recognized the importance of maintaining a strong connection with the nation's traditions and history. We delve into the creation of cultural institutions such as the Qatar National Library and the Katara Cultural Village, both of which serve as vibrant centers for learning, culture, and artistic expression. These landmarks house an extensive collection of books and historical artifacts, offering a glimpse into Qatar's rich heritage and its connections to the broader Arab and Islamic world.

The chapter also delves into Qatar's emergence as a global player in the world of sports. The decision to host the 2022 FIFA World Cup, while steeped in controversy and challenges, symbolizes Qatar's determination to make its mark on the international stage. We explore the massive infrastructure projects and cutting-edge stadium designs that are transforming the Qatari landscape and making the nation a focal point for international sporting events.

The ambitious goal of building a sustainable and innovative city for the World Cup, while addressing concerns about labor rights and climate, underscores the intricate web of challenges Qatar faces in pursuing its global ambitions.

As Chapter 5 unfolds, we witness Qatar's rising influence in regional and global politics, as the nation takes on an increasingly active role in international diplomacy and humanitarian efforts. The blockade imposed by neighboring countries in 2017 and Qatar's subsequent diplomatic outreach highlight the complexity of the regional dynamics in the Middle East.

The story of Qatar's growing role in mediating conflicts and providing humanitarian aid offers insight into the nation's aspirations to foster peace and stability in the region, further underlining its global ambitions.

"Building a Cultural Oasis" is a chapter that explores Qatar's multifaceted efforts to become a global hub for education, culture, and sports. It showcases the nation's dedication to shaping a brighter future while navigating the intricacies of global influence and the challenges that come with it.

6

The Diplomatic Dance - Qatar's Role in Regional and Global Affairs

In Chapter 6, we dive into Qatar's intricate and often delicate role in regional and global politics. This chapter explores how this tiny nation, despite its small geographical size, has managed to exert an outsized influence in a turbulent and complex geopolitical landscape.

Qatar's foreign policy is marked by strategic pragmatism and a commitment to diplomacy. The chapter opens with an examination of Qatar's approach to international relations, characterized by its delicate balancing act between major global powers and its steadfast efforts to maintain its sovereignty.

One of the defining moments in Qatar's recent history is the 2017 blockade imposed by several neighboring countries, including Saudi Arabia, the United Arab Emirates, and Bahrain. This diplomatic crisis had a profound impact on Qatar's foreign relations and regional standing. We explore the causes and consequences of the blockade, as well as Qatar's response, which was marked by resilience, assertiveness, and a quest for multilateral diplomacy to resolve the crisis.

The blockade, in many ways, revealed Qatar's strength in navigating regional politics and building international alliances. We delve into Qatar's role in the Gulf Cooperation Council (GCC) and its efforts to restore unity within the organization. The chapter also discusses the broader context of regional rivalries and conflicts, such as the war in Yemen and the complex relationships between the Gulf states and Iran.

Qatar's proactive diplomacy extends beyond its immediate region. We explore the nation's role in mediating conflicts, such as the Afghan peace process and the Darfur crisis, showcasing Qatar's aspiration to promote peace and stability on a global scale.

The chapter also examines Qatar's commitment to humanitarian causes and international development. We delve into the nation's contributions to organizations like the United Nations and its investments in global development projects, particularly in impoverished regions of Africa and Asia. These initiatives underscore Qatar's role as a responsible global citizen and its dedication to addressing the pressing challenges of our time.

Qatar's military and defense policies are another critical aspect of its foreign relations. The chapter discusses the establishment of the U.S. Al Udeid Air Base and the nation's commitment to regional security, as well as its collaboration with various Western military forces. Qatar's defense alliances, coupled with its efforts to build a strong defense sector, are vital components of its foreign policy and its role in maintaining regional stability.

Throughout Chapter 6, we witness the intricacies of Qatar's diplomacy and the nation's efforts to navigate the ever-evolving dynamics of the Middle East and the broader international arena. Qatar's role as a mediator, its commitment to humanitarian causes, and its contributions to global development projects all reflect the nation's determination to play a meaningful role in shaping a more stable and prosperous world.

"The Diplomatic Dance" is a chapter that underscores Qatar's nuanced approach to regional and global politics, showcasing the nation's influence and its aspirations to contribute positively to the complex web of international relations.

7

Challenges and Controversies - Qatar's Path to Sustainable Opulence

In Chapter 7, we delve into the challenges and controversies that have punctuated Qatar's remarkable journey toward opulence. Despite its meteoric rise and strategic vision, the nation has faced a range of complex issues that have drawn international scrutiny and sparked internal debates.

One of the central issues explored in this chapter is the treatment of expatriate laborers who have played a vital role in the nation's development. Qatar's rapid growth and infrastructure projects have attracted a significant expatriate workforce. We investigate the concerns and controversies surrounding labor rights, working conditions, and living conditions for these laborers. Qatar's response to these issues, including labor law reforms and efforts to improve workers' conditions, is examined, as is the nation's commitment to human rights on the global stage.

Environmental sustainability is another pressing concern. The rapid urbanization and infrastructure development in Qatar have raised questions about the environmental impact. We delve into the initiatives and challenges

Qatar faces in managing its natural resources, conserving its unique desert ecosystem, and addressing climate change. The drive to balance rapid economic growth with environmental responsibility is at the core of Qatar's commitment to sustainability.

The blockade imposed by neighboring countries in 2017 remains a significant geopolitical challenge. We explore the ongoing diplomatic efforts to resolve the crisis, as well as the effects on Qatar's economy, politics, and social fabric. The chapter also delves into the enduring regional tensions and rivalries that have persisted in the Gulf, with Qatar navigating a complex regional landscape.

Media freedom and the role of Al Jazeera, the influential Qatari news network, are also subjects of scrutiny. We examine the controversy surrounding media coverage and the challenges of maintaining independent journalism in a region marked by political conflicts and censorship.

Chapter 7 delves into Qatar's evolving stance on social issues, including efforts to promote gender equality and the rights of women in the workplace and society. The chapter also explores Qatar's engagement with global issues, such as countering extremism and terrorism, and the role of the nation in humanitarian efforts.

Amid these challenges and controversies, Qatar continues to build its brand as a global destination for culture, sports, and business. The chapter explores Qatar's ongoing investments in world-class events, such as the FIFA World Cup and the Qatar Economic Forum, reflecting its ambition to become a global meeting place and a hub for innovation and trade.

Chapter 7 paints a comprehensive picture of the complex issues that have emerged as Qatar has risen to global prominence. It illustrates the nation's capacity to respond to challenges, adapt to a changing world, and maintain its commitment to responsible development, all while striving for a more sustainable and inclusive opulence.

8

Qatar's Vision for the Future - Navigating Uncertainties

Chapter 8 delves into Qatar's vision for the future as it navigates the uncertainties of a rapidly changing world. The nation's leaders and its people have set their sights on sustainable development, innovation, and long-term prosperity, even as global dynamics continue to evolve.

The foundation for Qatar's future, as outlined in Qatar National Vision 2030, emphasizes diversification of the economy, investment in human capital, and environmental sustainability. The chapter explores how Qatar is working toward these goals, with a focus on promoting entrepreneurship and innovation. We examine the burgeoning startup scene, incubators, and initiatives designed to foster a culture of creativity and enterprise.

As Qatar continues to build its knowledge-based economy, the nation's leaders are investing in research and development. The establishment of the Qatar Science & Technology Park and the Qatar Foundation for Education, Science and Community Development are emblematic of these efforts. We delve into the initiatives aimed at nurturing homegrown innovation and advancing Qatar's technological capabilities.

In this chapter, we also examine Qatar's push for economic diversification beyond hydrocarbons. The nation has invested heavily in industries like finance, information technology, healthcare, and education. We explore how these sectors are contributing to Qatar's economic resilience and long-term sustainability.

The chapter delves into the evolution of the Qatari financial sector and its aspirations to become a global financial hub. We look at the development of the Qatar Financial Centre, the Qatar Stock Exchange, and the ongoing reforms to attract foreign investment and foster a thriving financial ecosystem.

Infrastructure development remains a cornerstone of Qatar's vision for the future, especially as it prepares to host the 2022 FIFA World Cup. We explore the ambitious plans for transportation, stadiums, and accommodations, which are designed to make the World Cup a sustainable and memorable event.

Education and research continue to be paramount in Qatar's vision for the future. We discuss the nation's partnerships with prestigious universities, its investments in science and technology, and the nurturing of a new generation of thinkers, innovators, and leaders.

Chapter 8 also delves into Qatar's role in global efforts to combat climate change. The nation's initiatives to reduce carbon emissions, increase energy efficiency, and promote renewable energy sources underscore its commitment to sustainability and responsible development.

While Qatar pursues its ambitious goals, it is also increasingly active on the international stage. We explore the nation's role in global diplomacy, humanitarian efforts, and peacekeeping missions, reflecting its aspiration to contribute positively to a world in flux.

As we journey through Chapter 8, we see that Qatar's vision for the future is characterized by adaptability, innovation, and a commitment to sustainability. The nation continues to navigate the complex global landscape, as it strives to transform its opulence into a model for a prosperous, inclusive, and resilient future.

9

Qatar's Place in a Globalized World - Challenges and Opportunities

Chapter 9 delves into Qatar's role and aspirations in a rapidly globalizing world. The nation's leaders and people recognize the importance of staying connected, both regionally and internationally, while facing a dynamic array of challenges and opportunities.

One of the central themes explored in this chapter is Qatar's role in regional and global trade. The nation's strategic location and world-class infrastructure make it a natural hub for trade and logistics. We investigate the initiatives to establish Qatar as a global trade player, the development of the Hamad Port, and the expansion of Hamad International Airport, all of which are essential components of Qatar's ambitions in the field.

The chapter also delves into Qatar's commitment to connectivity through its national airline, Qatar Airways. We explore the airline's rapid growth, its global network, and its award-winning service, reflecting Qatar's aspiration to become a key player in the global aviation industry.

Qatar's foray into global investments is another critical aspect of this chapter. We discuss the nation's sovereign wealth fund, the Qatar Investment Authority, and its efforts to diversify investments across various sectors and geographies. The chapter investigates the strategic vision behind Qatar's investments, including high-profile acquisitions and collaborations with international partners.

In the realm of culture and education, Qatar continues to strive for a global presence. We explore Qatar's initiatives to promote its culture and heritage worldwide, from museum exhibitions and cultural festivals to the sponsorship of academic research and scholarships.

The chapter also discusses Qatar's commitment to international development and humanitarian efforts. We delve into the nation's partnerships with international organizations and its contributions to projects that aim to alleviate suffering and promote sustainable development in crisis-affected regions.

As Qatar expands its global influence, it also confronts global challenges. The chapter investigates how the nation navigates issues such as cybersecurity, international terrorism, and international crises, while promoting stability and peace in the region and beyond.

The ongoing changes in the global energy landscape present another set of challenges and opportunities. As the world transitions to cleaner energy sources, we explore how Qatar is positioning itself to remain a leading player in the global energy market, particularly in the field of liquefied natural gas (LNG).

As we journey through Chapter 9, we witness Qatar's ambitions to shape the global landscape while addressing the complexities of a rapidly globalizing world. The nation's focus on trade, investment, connectivity, and cultural exchange is a testament to its vision of playing an influential role in the interconnected world of the 21st century.

10

Shaping the Future - Qatar's Legacy and Beyond

In the final chapter of our exploration into Qatar's journey, we reflect on the nation's enduring legacy, its continued pursuit of innovation and sustainability, and the path that lies ahead.

We begin by examining the nation's legacy as a global cultural and intellectual hub. Qatar's investments in education, research, and cultural preservation have borne fruit, leaving an indelible mark on the world. We explore the enduring impact of institutions like Education City, the Qatar National Library, and the Katara Cultural Village, as well as Qatar's contributions to art, literature, and knowledge sharing on the global stage.

The legacy of Qatar's World Cup preparation is also a focal point in this chapter. As the world's attention turns to the 2022 FIFA World Cup, we investigate how Qatar's innovative stadium designs, sustainable infrastructure projects, and global media coverage have not only reshaped the tournament but also set new standards for hosting major sporting events.

Sustainability and environmental responsibility continue to be at the forefront of Qatar's vision for the future. We explore the nation's efforts to combat climate change, reduce carbon emissions, and conserve its unique desert ecosystem, exemplifying its commitment to a greener and more sustainable future.

Chapter 10 also delves into Qatar's evolving role in regional and global affairs. We discuss how the nation is positioned to continue its diplomatic efforts, mediating conflicts, promoting peace, and contributing to international development and humanitarian initiatives. Qatar's aspiration to be a responsible global citizen remains at the heart of its foreign policy.

Qatar's commitment to innovation and technology is also explored in this chapter. We examine how the nation's investments in research and development, startup incubators, and initiatives to foster creativity and entrepreneurship are shaping a new era of innovation and progress.

The chapter discusses the evolving role of Qatar's financial sector and the nation's aspiration to become a global financial hub. We explore how these ambitions are driving economic diversification, foreign investment, and financial sector growth.

As Qatar's journey unfolds, it becomes evident that the nation is not only shaping its own future but also contributing to the betterment of the world. The chapter reflects on the challenges and opportunities that Qatar faces in a rapidly changing global landscape, highlighting the nation's resilience and adaptability.

In closing, Chapter 10 invites the reader to ponder Qatar's unique position as a nation that has transformed itself into a global powerhouse in the span of a few decades. The narrative encapsulates the nation's opulence, vision, and commitment to innovation, sustainability, and positive global impact. Qatar's journey continues, and its legacy stands as an example of what can be achieved when ambition, vision, and dedication converge to shape a brighter future for generations to come.

11

Qatar's Global Impact - A Beacon of Hope and Progress

In this final chapter of our journey through Qatar's history and evolution, we explore the nation's global impact as a beacon of hope and progress. Qatar has not only shaped its own destiny but also made a positive difference on the international stage.

This chapter begins by reflecting on Qatar's influence in fostering regional peace and stability. The nation's role as a mediator in various conflicts and its dedication to diplomatic solutions contribute to a more peaceful Middle East. We delve into specific initiatives and diplomatic efforts that have helped build bridges and resolve tensions in the region.

Qatar's commitment to humanitarian causes takes center stage as we examine the nation's involvement in providing aid and relief in crisis-affected regions. We explore the nation's partnerships with international organizations and its contributions to projects aimed at alleviating suffering and promoting sustainable development, particularly in conflict zones.

Environmental sustainability remains a critical focus in this chapter, as Qatar continues to pioneer clean energy solutions and advocate for climate action on the global stage. We investigate how the nation is addressing climate change, reducing carbon emissions, and driving innovation in the energy sector, contributing to global efforts to combat environmental challenges.

Qatar's vision for a knowledge-based economy and a culture of innovation is explored in-depth. We examine the nation's investments in research and development, technology, and entrepreneurship, showcasing Qatar's aspirations to become a global hub for innovation, technology, and knowledge sharing.

The chapter also discusses Qatar's evolving role in shaping the global energy landscape. As the world transitions to cleaner energy sources, we explore how Qatar is positioning itself to remain a leader in the global energy market, particularly in the field of liquefied natural gas (LNG).

We conclude with a reflection on the profound and lasting impact Qatar has had on the world stage. The nation's journey from a modest desert enclave to a global powerhouse, its commitment to sustainability and responsible development, and its efforts to promote peace, stability, and progress are celebrated as a source of inspiration for nations worldwide.

Chapter 11 invites the reader to contemplate the significance of Qatar's remarkable journey and its role in shaping a brighter and more hopeful future for the world. Qatar's global impact is not only a testament to its opulence and ambitions but also a beacon of hope and progress for the entire international community.

12

A Vision Realized - Qatar's Enduring Legacy

As we embark on the final chapter of Qatar's captivating narrative, we find ourselves at a point of reflection and celebration. Chapter 12 delves into the enduring legacy of Qatar, a nation that has transformed itself from the humble beginnings of a desert enclave to a global powerhouse.

This chapter begins with a retrospective glance at the key milestones of Qatar's journey. It revisits the nation's origins, the discovery of oil, the visionary leadership that shaped its destiny, and the challenges and opportunities that defined its path.

We explore the lasting impact of Qatar's investments in education, culture, and innovation, which have not only enriched the nation but also contributed to the global knowledge pool. The institutions of Education City, the cultural landmarks, and the commitment to fostering creativity and entrepreneurship all stand as a testament to Qatar's dedication to knowledge and progress.

A VISION REALIZED - QATAR'S ENDURING LEGACY

The enduring legacy of the 2022 FIFA World Cup is a focal point in this chapter. We reflect on the impact of the World Cup in transforming not only Qatar's infrastructure but also the global sporting landscape. The sustainable stadiums, state-of-the-art transportation systems, and the world's gaze upon Qatar symbolize the nation's vision realized.

Sustainability and environmental responsibility remain at the heart of Qatar's legacy. The chapter explores the nation's commitment to combating climate change and protecting its unique desert ecosystem, serving as a role model for responsible environmental stewardship.

The chapter also discusses the legacy of Qatar's role in regional and global diplomacy. We reflect on the nation's mediation efforts, its commitment to humanitarian causes, and its contributions to international development and peacekeeping initiatives. Qatar's legacy as a responsible global citizen continues to shape a more peaceful and stable world.

In this chapter, we celebrate Qatar's achievements in the financial sector and its vision for continued economic diversification. We explore how the nation's investments, partnerships, and initiatives are leaving a lasting impact on the global financial landscape.

The narrative closes with a reflection on Qatar's global impact as a beacon of hope and progress, a nation that has used its resources, ambition, and vision to make a positive difference in the world.

Chapter 12 serves as a testament to Qatar's enduring legacy, its contributions to global progress, and its continued journey toward a brighter and more sustainable future. It is an ode to a nation that has not only realized its vision but has become an inspiration for nations worldwide.

13

Summary

"Qatar's Golden Sands: A Tale of Opulence and Intrigue" is a comprehensive exploration of Qatar's history, transformation, and its global impact. Across twelve chapters, the narrative traces the nation's journey from its humble beginnings to its status as a global powerhouse, highlighting key milestones, challenges, and achievements along the way.

Chapter 1 sets the stage with an introduction to Qatar, its culture, and its remarkable transformation. Chapter 2 delves into the ancient roots of the nation, emphasizing its heritage as a trading hub and the influences of foreign powers. Chapter 3 explores the pearling industry, piracy, and power struggles that characterized Qatar's history.

Chapter 4 focuses on Qatar's transformation with the discovery of oil, visionary leadership, and the emergence of a modern state. Chapter 5 delves into Qatar's commitment to education, culture, and sports, showcasing the nation's ambition to become a global hub for knowledge and entertainment.

Chapter 6 discusses Qatar's role in regional and global diplomacy, the 2017 blockade, and the nation's contributions to peace and humanitarian efforts. Chapter 7 delves into the challenges and controversies Qatar faces, such as

SUMMARY

labor rights, environmental sustainability, and the impact of the blockade.

Chapter 8 explores Qatar's vision for the future, emphasizing innovation, diversification, and sustainability. Chapter 9 delves into Qatar's role in global trade, investments, and connectivity, showcasing its ambition to become a global player.

Chapter 10 reflects on Qatar's legacy and its contributions to regional peace, humanitarian efforts, and environmental sustainability. Chapter 11 focuses on Qatar's global impact in fields like diplomacy, humanitarian efforts, and environmental sustainability.

Chapter 12 concludes the narrative with a reflection on Qatar's enduring legacy, including its achievements in education, culture, innovation, the 2022 FIFA World Cup, and its continued global influence as a responsible global citizen.

The story of Qatar's journey is one of remarkable transformation, ambition, and a commitment to knowledge, sustainability, and global progress. It is a tale of opulence, diplomacy, and a vision realized, with Qatar emerging as a beacon of hope and progress on the international stage.

www.ingramcontent.com/pod-product-compliance
Lightning Source LLC
LaVergne TN
LVHW010442070526
838199LV00066B/6154